"their is a Cannal going throu from Falkirk to Edinburgh and they are cutting a tunal belaw grany from west side of our moar all the way to the glen burn about half a mill at Eduard McKenzes cannal will be about 100 feet belaw the surface they sunk pits about 100 yards from each other to the level of the cannal and then cut east and west till they met belaw taking all the stuff up by windlasts and when they met they cut it the proper size and raise the stuff out at the mouthes of the tunal a very great undertaking a great deal of Irish men came over and is employed at it and several accident has happened at it and 2 was killed by the face of the brea faling down on them few of our countrymen is at it as in general they cannot stand the work they are mostly irish young men and a bad set they are their is to be a bridge at Linlithgow which is to cost a number of £1000."

Letter from Falkirk to New York, Sept. 20th. 1818

their is a Cannal.

J. K. ALLAN

This publication by Falkirk Museums on the Canals of the
area links the basic history of these canals with contemporary
accounts of ways in which the canals, both during and after
construction, affected the lives of the people who worked
upon them or lived close to them. As many of these
contemporary accounts are contained in the archives of
Falkirk Museum, this publication serves the secondary purpose
of bringing documents to life and of making a local museum
more meaningful to the people whose support it enjoys.

Should interest in canals be stimulated, more detailed works
are available and reference will be made to them. For those
who are statistically minded, some of the facts and figures
are included in an appendix.

ISBN 0 9502250 5 3

growth of an idea

An Act for making and maintaining a navigable Canal from the Firth or River of Forth, at or near the mouth of the River Carron, in the county of Stirling, to the Firth or River of Clyde, at or near a place called Dalmuir Burnfoot, in the county of Dumbarton : ....

This was the title of the first Act of Parliament relating to what would become the Forth & Clyde canal. The act is dated 1768. While this might seem a proper point in time to begin an account of the canals of the eastern part of Central Scotland, the story does not begin here, for the idea of a canal joining Forth and Clyde is said to begin with Charles II who proposed opening a passage for warships. Certainly in 1726 Alexander Gordon, "an engineer of repute", was commissioned to survey the route, but reported that "the facility of effecting it greatly surpasses the idea which I had of it". In 1759, Lord Napier employed Mr. MacKell to lay down the plan of a canal. MacKell's report in 1764 was so favourable that "The Honourable the Board of Trustees for encouraging Fisheries, Manufacturers, and Improvements in Scotland", immediately employed John Smeaton to make the necessary surveys and to prepare estimates. Smeaton, a Yorkshire engineer who had recently completed the Eddystone lighthouse, prepared a report recommending a route from the River Carron to the Clyde at Yoker Burn, at an estimated cost of £147,337. Further delay was incurred, while Smeaton refuted the objections of Brindley and other engineers, and while consideration was given to a smaller project linking Glasgow and the Forth. However, Smeaton's plan was finally accepted. Digging began near the Grange Burn on June 10th. 1768.

Support for and opposition to the proposed canal are worth investigation, for these different attitudes display the diverse currents of interest which were alive in contemporary Scotland. The preamble to the Act of 1768 claimed that the canal would help "the improvement of the adjacent lands, the relief of the poor, and the preservation of the public roads;"

and it should be kept in mind that an account of the River Forth at this time could refer to "a very extensive general trade" and to the "vast quantity of merchandise which must necessarily pass along it, to supply the richest and most populous parts of Scotland". The canal gained support from the recently established Carron Iron Company because the eastern entry was fixed at Carronshore; equally from the tobacco merchants of Glasgow who saw in the canal an opportunity to facilitate re-export of American tobacco to the continent of Europe, with whom the ports of the Forth had enjoyed a considerable trade for many years. The latter were displeased by Smeaton's plan which by-passed their city, but were appeased by an insertion in the Act which allowed for "a collateral cut from the (Forth and Clyde) canal to the city of Glasgow". With two major exceptions the idea of a canal linking Forth and Clyde was supported by the merchants of most of the eastern counties of Scotland, who saw some advantage in being linked to "the extensive manufacturing districts around Glasgow and Paisley, and with the western parts of England and Scotland, and with Ireland".

The first of these exceptions was Bo'ness, for the merchants of Bo'ness saw the importance of their port threatened. Between 1750 and 1780 Bo'ness was one of the most thriving towns in Scotland, ranking the third largest seaport. Their opposition, argued from a position of established trading success, was similarly recognized in the Act by a clause allowing for a canal link from Carronshore to Bo'ness, but although work was started in 1783 by an independant company their original £8,000 capital was exhausted by the end of that year. A further £12,000 almost completed an aqueduct over the River Avon and the cutting of the canal from there to within a mile of Bo'ness, but when a further survey by Whitworth in 1789 estimated cost of completion at £17,763, it was finally agreed in 1796 that "it was expedient to abandon the canal". Within a very few years the fears of the Bo'ness merchants would be substantiated. The other source of major opposition came from the City of

proposed canal at Sealock (Grangemouth).

traces of the Bo'ness Canal near Bo'ness .

5

Edinburgh. A petition against the Bill, whose signatories included the Lord Provost, Magistrates and Town Council of Edinburgh, asked Parliament to postpone action on the "partial and local" scheme, so that plans could be drawn up for a "proper canal" which would serve national and universal interests. One writer in the contemporary press wrote of the "little despicable scheme of the Glasgow merchants" for "a ditch, a gutter, a mere puddle", which would serve the purposes of trade but not those of "magnificence and national honour". However articulate the opposition from Edinburgh might be, it would be some time before Parliamentary assent was given to the construction of the Edinburgh & Glasgow Union Canal. When the Act providing for a canal from "near the City of Edinburgh" to join the Forth and Clyde Canal "at or near Lock 16 opposite to Camelon House" received its final reading in June 1817, the latter was already a viable concern, and the primary objective of the Union Canal was less "to effect an inland communication between the cities of Edinburgh and Glasgow", more to provide a service to the former "in consequence of the increased facilities afforded to the transit of lime, coal, stone etc".

Glenfuir, showing route of canal, 1849.

Callendar Estate, to show objectionable effect of proposed canal.

land and water

Two aspects of planning had to be dealt with before any canal
construction could begin. These were acquisition of land and
availability of water. The Company of Proprietors of the
Forth and Clyde Navigation were empowered "to purchase and
acquire lands for the purpose of forming and maintaining a
canal from the River and Firth of Forth to the Firth and River
of Clyde", similar powers being later granted to the Union
Canal company. Problems of acquisition of land for the Forth
and Clyde Canal were to be relatively minor. Clauses in the
later Act which restrained the company from using land
belonging to William Forbes of Callendar, and from taking
the canal too close to the houses of prominent landowners were
to prove expensive for the proprietors of the Union Canal. The
countryside through which the Union Canal ran contained
many long-established estates, many of whose owners objected
to the presence of the canal workmen near their homes. The
owner of Glenfuir House overcame this problem by forcing
the company to buy his entire estate for 12,000 guineas. The
need to avoid the Callendar estate pushed the canal south of
Falkirk and involved taking the canal through a half-mile long
tunnel.

Water supply was the second determining factor in canal
construction. The Forth and Clyde Canal Company were
authorised to draw water from the Rivers Carron, Endrick, and
Kelvin, and from all rivers and lochs within 10 miles of the
Canal, provided they did not diminish water-supply to the
mills on the Carron and Kelvin. Similarly, authority was given
to the Union canal for reservoirs on Cobbinshaw Bog, for
feeders from the Avon and Almond, and for water to be taken
from a number of streams near the route. Water requirements
were based on the ubiquitous factor of "normal availability",
which might be read as "reasonable supply". Problems were
to arise later when, in times of drought, a reasonable supply of
water was unavailable.

There was a relation in canal design between the highest
summit level, the dimensions of the locks, which in turn

determined the size of barges which could operate, the antici-
pated volume of traffic, and the volume of water held in the
reservoirs. These considerations are apparent in the report of
Robert Whitworth when, in 1785, he prepared a survey for
completion of the Forth and Clyde canal from Stockingfield
to the Clyde. "There is another point of great importance to
be enquired into and that is the additional supplies of water
which will be necessary, when the western locks are made
down to the river Clyde, and an increase of trade upon the
Canal, which may be expected when the Canal is completed
from sea to sea.

It is not my business at present to enquire what the amount
of the present supplies are, but to point out where and how
an additional quantity of water may be procured, adequate
to the consumption that may be required for lockage, leakage
through the lock gates and banks, and exhalation. What the
real quantity that may be required for these purposes will be
is very uncertain, as it depends upon so many circumstances,
as the quantity of trade, etc." Various techniques were
employed to secure water supplies. An 1831 account of the
Canals tells that, on the Union Canal "there is a feeder of more
than three miles in length, taken from below the junction of
the Linthouse and Almond rivers, which crosses the latter
river by a suspension aqueduct; and between which and the
aqueduct over the Almond River there are three tunnels, one
of which is more than half a mile in length."

When provision of water had been made, supplies had to be
conserved. "The length of the (Union) canal is thirty miles,
the depth of the water 5 feet, and is on one level from
Edinburgh to its western extremity, where it falls 110 feet, in
one series of locks, into the Forth and Clyde canal". It was
more economical of water supplies to dig cuts, or tunnel, or
to build aqueducts in order to create long level stretches of
water and arrange locks in series.

The most difficult engineering feat was the building of the
Union Canal tunnel through Prospect Hill which, according to
engineer Hugh Baird's specifications, was "about 690 yards in
length, the dimensions of the Tunnel to be 13 feet of waterway
and 5 feet of track-path, making 18 feet in width; the height to
be 6ft. 6 inches from canal-bottom to top bank level, and 12
feet high above top bank level at least." The letter quoted
elsewhere shows that the local people were well-informed.

Problems of canal construction apart, when the canals were
completed they were a continuous source of interest and
wonder to visitors to the area. These impressions are summed
up by the writer of a letter to the Scots Magazine in 1805:
"The canal was to me an object of great curiosity, having
never seen it or anything on the same scale. Here it is carried
above the road, and the traveller in passing has the sensation
of water rolling and vessels sailing over his head. (This where
Camelon Bridge was later built.) On mounting to the banks, I
found that one vessel had just passed the locks above the
bridge, but another appeared in sight, which soon afforded me
an opportunity of observing the whole process, to me highly
interesting, though needless to describe. The breadth of the
water, the opening and shutting the massy gates of the locks,
with the vessels which glided smoothly and silently along,
presented an interesting spectacle and conveyed the agreeable
image of genius and industry directed to ends of extensive
public usefulness."

Union Canal Tunnel from the west.

Almond Aqueduct from the south-west.

working conditions

At an early Committee meeting, held at the Exchange Coffee House in Edinburgh, after the appointment of Smeaton as Head Engineer at £500 per annum and MacKell as Sub-Engineer at £315 per annum, MacKell was ordered to engage workmen. The wages of labourers were not to exceed 10p per day, and the overseer was to be paid the "lowest weekly wage possible".

Irish and Highland labour was imported, particularly the former. Irish labour seems to have been preferred because of the tendency of Highland labour to return home to agricultural work at the appropriate seasons. There are accounts of fights breaking out between the two groups, disturbances often attributed to public-houses "whose doors were open at all hours, Sunday not excepting, for giving drink to the men." People living near construction work on the canal complained of periodic disturbances, including the playing of bagpipes in the middle of the night.

The system of sub-contracting was prevalent. Contractors seem to have been paid from 3½ to 14 pence per cubic yard for excavating "stuff", a figure which varied with the nature of the material to be excavated. It is not quite clear what the men at the bottom of the sub-contracting pyramid were paid, but living conditions were rudimentary. An 1822 account described the contemporary scene. "Along the banks of the Union Canal certain edifices have been erected. These are huts erected by Irish labourers, upon some few vacant spots of ground belonging to the Canal proprietors, and are pointed out to strangers in the passage boats as great curiosities. Each, of course, is more wretched than another, and presents a picture of squalid poverty which is new to people on this side of the Channel. One of them, with the exception of a few sticks, is composed entirely of rotten straw; its dimensions would not suffice for a pig-sty, and its form is that of a beehive, only it is more conical. The smoke which does not escape at the door penetrates through every part of the structure, which thus presents at all times the appearance of a

page from Wilson's log, 1843.

sketch from engineer's notebook of tools and hopper barges.

nd it is thought the night being extremely dark and
he had taken the Canal for the Road. three Boys
were standing on Randel Bridge observed him pass
and heard the Plunge they made the alarm but
before assistance, could be got it was half an hour
before his body was got out

Robert Jones one of our Labourers has
got himself severely hurt in blasting the Stone
in the bottom of the Dock one of his fingers
was blown off and his head severely injured

Wednesday 25th

Carpenters imployed in Shelving the Lower Gal

a Long Shafted Spade with one set up Side

a long Shafted Spade with two Sides set up contrived for lifting
Clay into Small Sp...

a Spade or Wedge with a Strong Shaft to be Driven with Mall

hay-rick on fire. A Hottentot kraal, in comparison with it, is a palace. In the midst of so much misery, the children appear healthy and frolicsome, and the men and women contented and happy".

Because of the nature of the work of canal construction, and the number of men employed at it - in 1789 there were 14 contractors, 25 carpenters, 81 Quarrymen, 130 masons and 419 labourers - it is not surprising that there were a considerable number of injuries. In 1796 the Forth and Clyde Canal Company, and in 1818 the Union Canal Company, decided to subscribe to the Glasgow Royal Infirmary so that employees injured in future accidents would be entitled to treatment there. By the standards of the time this was a progressive arrangement, particularly if it is kept in mind that only in 1775 did an Act of Parliament amend the situation "whereas many colliers, coal-bearers, and slaters in Scotland are in a state of slavery or bondage", and until 1843 (and later) women and young children were employed to do arduous underground work in Scottish coal-mines. Nevertheless, accounts of accidents seem to accept their inevitability, and delay in obtaining treatment somewhat protracted. An engineer's log-book from 1843, when Grangemouth docks were being extended, reads: "Wed. 4th. Jan. One of Peter Feely's men met with a dangerous injury from a waggon passing over his body", and later, "Tues. 24th. Jan. Robert Jones one of our labourers got himself severely hurt in blasting stones in the bottom of the dock one of his fingers was blown off and his head severely injured". The arrangement with Glasgow Royal Infirmary still stood, but it was noon the following day before the injured man was put on a canal boat to be carried to Glasgow for treatment.

The arduous nature of the work of building the canals, and the living conditions of the workmen probably compared with the life of the ordinary home-dweller, in the same way as do working conditions on civil-engineering undertakings to-day. There is little evidence left of the presence in the area of large

16

Doctor's Wood, Bonnybridge.

numbers of expatriate labour, save in the tales which remain. Two of the Irish labourers who helped dig the Union Canal, named Burke and Hare, went on to achieve notoriety digging on other, more hallowed, fields. With the same macabre connections, Bonnybridge still has its Doctor's Wood, where reputedly bodies were surreptitiously stowed on canal-boats by night for shipment to the experimenting surgeons of Edinburgh.

GEORGII III. REGIS.

●●

Cap. xxix.

An Act for altering and amending an Act for making and maintaining a Navigable Canal from the *Lothian* Road near the City of *Edinburgh* to join the *Forth* and *Clyde* Navigation near *Falkirk* in the County of *Stirling*. [19th *May* 1819.]

WHEREAS an Act was passed in the Fifty-seventh Year of the Reign of His present Majesty, intituled *An Act for making and* 57 G. 3. c. 56. *maintaining a Navigable Canal from the* Lothian *Road near the* City *of* Edinburgh *to join the* Forth *and* Clyde *Navigation near* Falkirk *in the County of* Stirling ; and certain Persons were thereby incorporated for carrying the same into execution by the Name and Style of The *Edinburgh* and *Glasgow* Union Canal Company : And whereas it has been ascertained in the Course of the Operations now in progress on the said Canal, that the Line thereof laid down by the said Act may in several Places be materially improved : And whereas it is expedient that the said recited Act should be otherwise altered, amended, and enlarged ; but as these Purposes cannot be accomplished without the Aid and Authority of Parliament ; may it therefore please Your Majesty that it may be enacted ; and be it enacted by the King's most Excellent Majesty, by and with the Advice and Consent of the Lords Spiritual and

[*Local.*] 8 E Temporal,

legal problems

In public undertakings of this, for Scotland, unprecedented scale, it might be expected that the original and supplementary Acts of Parliament dealt with every conceivable difficulty, from powers to acquire land to mode of settlement of price. For example, money in excess of £200 was to be paid "with all conceivable speed" into the Bank of Scotland or Royal Bank of Scotland "under the direction and by the authority of the Court of Session" in cases where "lands, tenements or heritages" purchased belonged to "any incorporation, married woman, infant, lunatic or persons under any disability or incapacity." Perhaps because of this attention to detail which seemed to cope with every eventuality, the Company were able to claim in 1798 that they "believed they had more transactions in the form of arbitration, and fewer law-suits, than any society of undertakers in the kingdom". There were still occasions, both before and after completion of the two canals, which necessitated court action.

Sometimes this involved long delay in settlement though not in canal construction. One case, heard in court in 1798, eight years after the opening of the Forth and Clyde Canal, concerned the price of a section of land near the western end which had been cut ten years previously. The Company sought a reduction in the price of £50 per Scots acre paid for the land, arguing that the owner "fell upon a very ingenious contrivance to enhance, as he thought, the value of his ground by procuring an offer from a person entirely ignorant of the circumstances of that property, to convert it into a bleachfield, and to pay a very high rent for it on that account, which transaction never took effect; and the owner knew well that no such project could be executed". This land, they argued, could never have functioned as a bleachfield because of inadequate water supply. In reply, the owner argued that the Company, "for the sake of avoiding the many forms prescribed by the acts of parliament, for having the values of lands and damages ascertained by commissioners or juries, usually, if not always, resorted to the common mode of reference to three or four gentlemen of character".

Act of George III in respect of the Union Canal.

Producing contrary evidence, he argued that the evidence of
a shopkeeper, an exciseman, and a weaver, together with two
very respectable gentlemen" "cannot for a single moment be
put in competition with that of ten or twelve practical bleachers
who were much better able to judge of the water necessary for
a bleachfield". In showing how the Canal, by dividing his land
had rendered it unfit for this purpose, he asked the Court to
support the original price fixed and to award legal expenses
against the Company. The cost to the Company in this instance
was insignificant in relation to the subsequent settlement of
the negotiation between the Union Canal Company and the
owner of Glenfuir Estate, already referred to.

Apart from the relatively small number of disputes which
required settlement in court, the records of the Canal compan-
ies, maintained during their operative life, provide a source of
the diverse complaints which were from time to time
directed at them. In 1827, correspondence with Miss Dallas of
Gilmore Place, Edinburgh, complains of the pigs and cows kept
by the Keeper of the drawbridge. An examination of the
Keeper's house found that "he had erected a shed for cows,
with a boiler, a pig stye, and a shed for keeping their meat.
The space in front of his house was very dirty with Cow Dung
etc., and there was somewhat of an offensive smell from the
boiler". From the other end of the canal, a letter in 1827
from Reverend Andrew Sym of Kilpatrick stated that the
funds of the parish had been encroached on by funeral
expenses of persons drowned in the canal and for the support
of the widows and families of the deceased servants of the
company.

Given the scale of enterprise necessary to build and operate
the canals, such complaints were perhaps inevitable. Nevertheless, a contemporary Scots Magazine could refer to "one of
the most elegant, useful and convenient undertakings this
Kingdom has ever produced."

Keeper's House, Dalgrain Bridge, Grangemouth.

Lock Keeper's Cottage, lock 9.

operation and decline

The value of the canals to the community was illustrated even before the first canal was completed. By January 1775 the canal was filled and traffic was operating from the Forth to Stockingfield, though at this point work slowed down because of lack of funds and because Smeaton had resigned his post in 1773 and MacKell died in 1779. It should be kept in mind that at this time Scotland's roads were few and in poor condition, and alternative means of transporting goods in bulk non-existent. By 1784 the advent of peace in North America where war had led to a virtual collapse of Glasgow's tobacco trade, improved prospects for canal revenue. The Company was loaned a further £50,000 from forfeited estates of Jacobite supporters, and the following year Robert Whitworth was appointed chief engineer. In July 1790 the official open-ing ceremony was performed "in presence of a great crowd of spectators, by Archibald Spiers, Esq. of Elderslie" who "launched a hogshead of water of the river Forth into the Clyde as a symbol of joining the eastern and western seas together".

During the first thirty years of operation, under the chairman-ship of Lord Dundas of Kerse, canal revenue showed an overall increase from £6,835 in the first year to £49,974. There were fluctuations due to various circumstances. The Napoleonic Wars caused decreased revenue from the fishing-industry because of the Navy's demand for sailors and at the same time disrupted the Baltic trade; however, the number of vessels using the canal to avoid the danger of French warships when sailing around the North of Scotland increased. Severe frosts in 1820 closed the canal for a considerable time and cost £2,000 in lost revenue. Lord Dundas was not, however, with-out his critics, who commented adversely on "idle and unprofitable projects" such as the building, by William Symington in 1801-3, of the steam-engined paddle-driven "Charlotte Dundas". Designed to replace horses as the motive power for pulling barges, it proved its capabilities, but never entered service because the canal proprietors were afraid of the effects of its wash on the canal banks. More successful ventures instigated during this period were the

canal posters, 1834 and 35.

canal basin, Grangemouth.

Alteration of Hours.

Safe, Comfortable, & Cheap Travelling,

BETWEEN

ALLOA AND GLASGOW,

BY

STAGE COACH & CANAL GIG PASSAGE BOATS

On and after Monday the 6th October Current,
the Hours of Starting will be as follows:—

From ALLOA FERRY,	From Pt. Dundas, Glasgow,
At half past 5 morning,	At 7 o'Clock morning,
At 3 o'Clock afternoon.	At a Quarter past 4 afternoon.

TABLE of FARES,

Cabin of Boat and Inside of Coach, - -	5/
Cabin of Boat and Outside of Coach, - -	4/6
Steerage of Boat and Inside of Coach, -	4/
Steerage of Boat and Outside of Coach, -	3/6

No Allowance Payable to Boatmen or Coach-Driver.

Passengers leaving Alloa at half past 5 o'Clock morning, will be in Glasgow at 10 morning, and those leaving Alloa at 3 will be in Glasgow at 8 Evening, same time occupied in returning from Glasgow.

SEATS BOOKED AT THE

Steam Shipping Office, Forth Street, ALLOA,
91 Trongate, GLASGOW, and
Union Hotel No. 16, Passage Boat Office, Pt. Dundas Glasgow

Notice to Passengers to and from Kincardine.

As the above Coach runs by the way of AIRTH, CARRON, CARRON SHORE, BAINSFORD, and FALKIRK, and passes the New Road leading to Kincardine Ferry in about 30 minutes after leaving Alloa,—Passengers from KINCARDINE can go by this Conveyance.

FARES,—same as from Alloa.

An OMNIBUS starts from the CROSS, Glasgow, a quarter before the hour of the boats starting, & is waiting their arrival at Pt. Dundas.

Passengers leaving Dunfermline

at or before 11 o'Clock, by the RAILWAY OMNIBUS to CHARLESTOWN, and from thence by any of the Steamers to Alloa or Stirling, will be in good time for the CANAL COMPANY'S COACH AND BOATS, and land at Glasgow
At HALF the FARE by any other Conveyance.

Alloa, 3 October, 1836.   J. Lothian, Printer, Alloa.

ALTERATION of HOURS

OF THE

FORTH & CLYDE CANAL

SWIFT

Passenger Boats

To commence 1st October, 1835.

From Port-Dundas.	From Lock No. 16.
At 8 o'Clock, Morning.	At 7 o'Clock, Morning.
" 11 o'Clock, Forenoon.	" 12 o'Clock, Noon.
" 2 o'Clock, Afternoon.	" 3 o'Clock, Afternoon.
" 4½ o'Clock, Afternoon.	" 6 o'Clock, Evening.

CABIN, 3s.—STEERAGE, 2s.

Passengers for Edinburgh must go by the Boats at 8, 11, or 2 o'clock; for Stirling at 8, 11, or 4½; for Perth via Crief, &c. at 8; for Kinross, &c. at 11 Forenoon; for Alloa at 4½ Afternoon; and for Kirkaldy via Dunfermline at 8 o'clock morning.

Fares to these Places Very Moderate.

Canal Office, Port-Dundas,
Glasgow, 21st Sept., 1835.

AITKEN & CO. PRINTERS

passenger services begun in 1809, sailing by canal-boat from Port Dundas to Lock 16 and by connecting coach from there to Edinburgh; and the building, to the accompaniment of inquirers who asked if he really expected it to "soum" of the first iron vessel. The "Vulcan" was built for the Company by Thomas Wilson between 1817 and 1819 - and it continued to sail until 1873. Thomas Wilson later became superintendent for the Company during the construction of Grangemouth dock extensions.

The Edinburgh and Glasgow Union Canal was officially opened in May 1822, despite problems with landowners, financial difficulties exacerbated by the engineering problems of aqueducts, cuttings and a tunnel, and the opposition from Leith merchants and shipowners who saw in the Union Canal a means to enhance the importance of Grangemouth. For whatever reasons, and water supply may have been one, locks on the Union Canal were smaller than those on the Forth and Clyde, which meant that Union barges could traverse the Forth & Clyde but not necessarily vice-versa and could involve transhipment. One effect of its opening was to make Lock 16, where Union joined Forth & Clyde, a focal point for passenger and goods traffic, and for the development of industry. Within a very short time "Lock 16" appeared on maps as the name by which the surrounding district was referred to.

Horses remained the motive power for canal traffic for a considerable time after Symington's pioneering efforts, indeed for towing lighters right into this century. No steamboats were used on the canal, their birthplace, until 1826 when various means of propulsion were tried, and it was not until the adoption of the screw propellor in 1856 that the first regular steamboat, the "Thomas", came into operation. A communication from the Canal Office in 1862 tells that there were then the following steam-craft in operation - " 1 passenger boat, 1 ice-breaker, 2 goods boats carrying from 30 to 40 tons, 12 mineral scows carrying from 55 to 65 tons, 11 lighters carrying from 70 to 85 tons, and 7 from 100 to 120 tons".

The advent of steam power, however contained mixed blessings for the future of the canals. From 1842 the railways were competing for traffic and as early as 1857 the timber business of James Jones moved from Camelon to Larbert, because the latter offered better rail facilities.

Passenger traffic was the first to feel the effects of competition. Since the 1790s the Canal Company had had four track-boats which served mainly for carrying goods but had limited passenger accommodation. In 1809 two purpose-built passenger-boats began to operate between Lock 16 and Port Dundas, with a network of connecting coach services at either terminal. In 1818, a pamphlet urging the building of the Union Canal referred to "the cheapness and accommodation of these passage-boats, which are cleaner than any inn in Scotland, and where the passengers are sheltered from the cold and rain in the cabins, and from the heat of the sun by awnings over the deck - where they can indulge themselves with walking or sitting, and can read and write at their pleasure - contrasted with the crowding and jolting, the cold in winter, the want of air under rain, and the heat and dust in summer, that attended the inside journeys in the coaches, with the dangers and hardships of the outside coach-passengers - will always secure to the boats between Glasgow and Edinburgh, the same preference over the coaches, that the boats between Glasgow and Falkirk have always met with."

Canal-borne passenger-boats could compete successfully with horse-drawn coaches. Their advantages disappeared in the face of the railways. However, the passenger services on the Forth and Clyde Canal, leased to a private company, continued to operate until the 1880s, and the Queen steamers were introduced by James Aitken of Kirkintilloch in 1893. These offered pleasure sails, and the largest, the Gipsy Queen, continued to operate until 1939 by which time canal trips were being advertised as "a delightful change from road-travel".

The Union Canal was a less commercially-viable proposition, its completion in 1822 allowing only 20 years of operation before the opening of the Edinburgh-Glasgow railway, and seven years later it was taken over by the railway company. The Forth and Clyde, on the other hand, probably remained viable until World War I when Grangemouth, as well as other ports above the Forth Bridge, was closed to merchant shipping. In fact, during the last quarter of the 19th. century although the traffic in grain, salt, sugar, oil, flour, stones, slate and coal declined, tonnage in pig-iron and timber actually increased.

There is no simple explanation for the final decline in transport of goods, the World War I ports closure being the culmination of a number of factors. The railways had a major effect, first in attracting the transport of people and goods away from the canals, later in affecting the siting of industry. Glasgow turned from the Baltic to North America for grain; Grangemouth became an international port rather than a canal terminal; coasting steamers became too large for canal locks and established lines linked Liverpool in the west with East coast ports from Newcastle to Aberdeen. The closure of the canals - 1963 and 1965 for Forth and Clyde and Union Canals respectively - was not entirely unopposed. There was protest from fishing communities of the Forth whose small herring-boats still made use of the inter-sea canal, but given the small amount of traffic, commercial or pleasure, using the canal any argument was doomed to failure.

horse-drawn barge, Union Canal.

outing by barge from Lanark Road, Edinburgh, 1912.

present and future

To anyone familiar with the central area of Scotland it is
stating the obvious to say that the canals have left a unique
historical record on the ground.

First, the canal structures largely remain as a visible reminder,
from series of locks at Camelon and Bowling to the long
level stretch of the Union Canal leading into Edinburgh where
it still serves as an indispensible supplier of water to industry.
There are outstanding structures such as the aqueducts over
the Avon, Almond and Water of Leith; a bascule bridge at
Bowling and the unique lifting-gear at Fountainbridge; along
the Union Canal where every structure was built from local
stone there remains many bridges, the sides of the arches
showing the grooves made by tow-ropes, marker-posts and
milestones. There are, at Camelon and elsewhere, lock-
keepers' cottages, still occupied, and the remains of stables
which provided a change of horse for tracking the canal boats
and lighters; and the Union Inn still stands as a reminder of the
people who travelled and worked on the canals.

Second, continuing to bear witness to the influence the canals
had on the social and industrial development of the area, is the
way in which many industrial structures are situated on the
banks of the canals. Kirkintilloch has its granary; in the Falkirk
area are many still-functioning iron-foundries.
Grangemouth, of course, owes its industrial development to
being made a canal terminal and it is still a centre for the
timber industry. At various points on the canal banks are
modern industrial estates, no longer attracted by the transport
facilities of the canal, nor the railways, but whose presence is
a continuation of the industrial zoning created initially by the
canal.

From a historical background, which has been referred to by
contemporary accounts as an "agreeable image of genius and
industry directed to ends of extensive public usefulness" or
"an elegant, useful and convenient undertaking". the canals
have largely survived a phase of closure and partial in-filling.

bascule bridge and pleasure craft, Bowling.

Union Inn, Camelon.

The public usefulness of the canals appears to have come through a full cycle, now recognised in the statutory remit of the British Waterways Board. "In the waterways, this country possesses a priceless asset whose value will grow as the demand for leisure facilities intensifies."

This legislation gives support to the current body of opinion which seeks to have the canals of the populous and industrial area of Central Scotland restored and conserved, as a visual reminder of the social, industrial and economic heritage of the area, and as an immediate and accessible environment which can make a significant contribution to the leisure and recreation of present and future generations. The natural historian lends support to this argument by pointing out that the preservation of the canals will help to maintain the widest possible range of semi-natural environments in the Central Belt of Scotland, with slow-moving waters supporting rich habitats from aquatic communities, through transition zones on canal margins and fringing trees and shrubs.

In different ways, the Forth and Clyde and Union Canals may continue in the future, as in the past, to provide a response to the needs of the community.

	Forth and Clyde	Union	Bo'ness
Terminal points	Grangemouth - Bowling	Camelon - Edinburgh	Grangemouth
Date of Act under which work commenced	1768	1817	1768
Date opened	1790	1822	
Approximate cost	£330,000	£461,760	£20,000
Length	35 miles	11 miles	abandoned 1797
Maximum size of boats	66' x 19'8"	69' x 12'6"	
Number of locks	40	11	
Height of summit level above terminal point.	156 feet	110 feet	
Principal aqueducts (length and height)	Kelvin (400', 70')	Avon (810', 86') Almond (420', 76') Slateford (500', 75')	

acknowledgements

The list following indicates further reading available and serves as acknowledgement of sources of material contained in this publication :

Charles Hadfield (ed.)   *The Canals of the British Isles*
David & Charles, Newton Abbot
(series)

Jean Lindsay   *The Canals of Scotland*
David & Charles, Newton Abbot,
1968.

Joseph Priestley   *Priestley's Navigable Rivers and
Canals*
David & Charles Reprints (1969)

Original source material from the following archives :

NATIONAL LIBRARY OF SCOTLAND, George IV Bridge,
Edinburgh.
Scots Magazine
Glasgow Herald
Edinburgh Evening Courant
Edinburgh Evening Dispatch
SCOTTISH RECORD OFFICE, Register House, Princes Street,
Edinburgh.
Union Canal Minute Book.
BRITISH WATERWAYS BOARD, Old Basin, Applecross,
Glasgow.
Forth & Clyde Canal Minute Book.

Plans on p.4 and 15 by permission of Sir John Clerk, Bt.,
Penicuik House, Midlothian.

Thanks are also due to J. Howdle, Edinburgh, for considerable assistance and W. Stoddart, Falkirk, for use of letter which provides the title for this publication.

ALLAN, J.K.
THEIR IS A CANNAL
386.4809